Beat Procrastination

9 Surprising tips for taking action and getting stuff done

by

Grace C. Vale

Table of Content

BEAT
PROCRASTINATION
9 SURPRISING TIPS FOR TAKING ACTION AND
GETTING STUFF DONE
Beat
Procrastination
And Get Stuff
Done

Introduction

I grew up in the city with my parents and Siblings. I was intelligent, bright, and full of promise, yet I repeatedly fell short of my standards. My siblings have to crack up every time I claim I want to start doing something since I am such a chronic procrastinator. They were aware that I would never start, I can't blame them. I'll just say that without doing anything to support it.

However, I secretly aspire to be a proactive achiever.

I began my transformational journey by looking for assistance from the internet

I aspired to be a thriving entrepreneur as well as a successful writer, and my aspirations twinkled like far-off stars. However, my goals remained restricted to the walls of my head as the days turned into weeks and those into months.

My unwelcome traveling companion was procrastination, a specter that mumbled doubts and lured me into passivity.

There is always a light at the end of the tunnel, as they say. I came upon an article titled "The Science of Procrastination and How to Manage It" one sweltering Tuesday afternoon. Intrigued! I started a voyage of self-discovery under the wisdom of the article. I learned the importance of productivity and the thrill of concentrated effort as I read the book. I felt the bonds of procrastination lessen as each minute of focused work passed. What a

Wonder! I discovered how to break the pattern of waiting and embrace the momentum of action.

It all began with accepting and learning about oneself. I realized and recognized that procrastination is my issue, and that I needed to recover from it.

Today, my dreams shine brilliantly as constellations of success rather than lingering as faraway stars. Wow!

I'm going to share the Surprising 9 strategies I learned to combat procrastination and complete tasks through the Chapters of this book.

But first, let me explain what procrastination is.

The word "procrastination" conjures up images of lost chances, unfulfilled ambitions, and the nagging sense of not living up to one's potential. The impulse to put off responsibilities until later, even when we know we should be acting, is something we've all felt at some point in our lives. It's a behavior that looks illogical; after all, why do we put off doing things that are crucial or even necessary?

Procrastination is not laziness. It is an emotional regulation problem and can lead to stress.

Procrastination can lead to depression and depression can also lead to procrastination

We examine the psychology of procrastination in this book, "Beat Procrastination: 9 Surprising Tips for Taking Action and Getting Stuff Done," and practical methods to combat it. These suggestions are intended to give you a new perspective on approaching chores, managing your time, and eventually reclaiming control over your actions, whether you're a chronic procrastinator or someone trying to increase your productivity.

The nine Surprising tips offered here are each supported by research, practical examples, and doable tasks. These tips are unexpected because they dispel myths about productivity and explore the psychology of the individual, giving you a comprehensive strategy for overcoming procrastination. These techniques range from the two-minute rule, which encourages you to complete work in manageable chunks, to the power of mindfulness, which encourages proactive action.

Keep an open mind and be prepared to accept change as you go out on this procrastination-busting quest. Keep in mind that overcoming procrastination is about making progress, not attaining perfection. You'll gain momentum and change your approach to activities and objectives with each minor accomplishment.

The journey ahead won't always be simple, but it will be worthwhile. You'll have a complete arsenal after this book to combat procrastination, and you'll be well on your way to leading a more successful, fulfilling, and action-driven life. Let's dig in and learn the unexpected advice that will enable you to act and complete tasks like never before.

Do not
Procastinate
LATER IS
TOO LATE

Chapter One

Tip 1: Two-minute rule

Procrastination frequently thrives on the resistance we feel when facing a task. A wonderfully successful tactic to break through this reluctance and start action is the Two-Minute Rule.

Consider a messy workstation that is full of unfinished projects and impending deadlines. It might be difficult to even choose where to start due to the suffocating weight of these unfinished tasks. This is where the Two-Minute Rule excels because it alters the way you approach activities and gives your daily routine a feeling of urgency and achievement.

Breaking a task into Small Steps

The Two-Minute Rule's guiding idea is elegantly straightforward: if a work can be finished in two minutes or less, do it right away. Its genius is in its capacity to turn more difficult, intimidating jobs into manageable chunks of work. Our brain considers work manageable when it involves little effort and time, which lessens the psychological resistance associated with starting a significant task.

Think about the duty of answering emails. A cluttered inbox may make tasks seem overwhelming and encourage procrastination.

However, if you followed the Two-Minute Rule, you would respond to each email right away if it could be handled in that amount of time or less. This methodical, step-by-step procedure not only clears your inbox but also sparks a sense of achievement that encourages more participation.

Overcoming the inertia of Starting

Because of the perceived effort involved, the human mind frequently hesitates before beginning a job. This cognitive barrier, referred to as the "inertia of starting," can seriously reduce productivity. The Two-Minute Rule efficiently combats this inertia by encouraging the swift completion of inconsequentially brief activities.

By starting a task with just two minutes, you may get beyond the difficult psychological barrier that causes procrastination. Once you get going on a job, you'll probably stick with it for longer than the recommended two minutes since you'll be riding a wave of momentum that will carry you through to the end.

Implementing The Two-Minute Rule

Start by identifying the things you've been putting off to fully utilize the power of the Two-Minute Rule. These might be quick tasks, correspondence via email or phone, or even brief brainstorming sessions. Each activity should be evaluated to see if it can be finished in two minutes or less. Decide to start tackling it right away if you can.

This rule necessitates a mental adjustment. You are taking proactive action to complete chores as they come up rather than letting them pile up and consume you. Your perspective on projects will change as you constantly use the Two-Minute Rule. What was previously a hassle is now a chance to act quickly, giving you a sense of control and achievement.

Building Momentum and consistency

The Two-Minute Rule's capacity to foster momentum is among its most impressive features. You'll probably feel more encouraged to carry on once you start finishing things quickly one after the other. This momentum boosts your productivity and helps you complete your to-do list more quickly.

To fully profit from this guideline, consistency is crucial. Consider scheduling two-minute assignments throughout various periods of the day. These intervals might occur at the start of your workday, during brief breaks, or even toward the conclusion of the day. You may minimize the buildup of activities that cause procrastination by designing your schedule to allow for these little victories.

A Gateway for Productive Behavior

The Two-Minute Rule is a starting point for creating useful habits, not merely a technique. By responding quickly to activities regularly, you educate your brain to link action with an immediate reward. Your behavior progressively changes as a result of this reinforcement, and production ceases to be an exceptional feat and begins to become the norm.

The Two-Minute Rule's simplicity offers a novel method for overcoming procrastination in a world overflowing with diversions and complicated obligations. The Two-Minute Rule may completely change how you approach productivity in your daily life. This tactic enables the completion of multiple modest chores and cultivates a proactive mentality that extends to more significant activities by transforming avoidance into action through its simple beauty.

You get the ability to overcome starting-related lethargy and turn difficult undertakings into doable actions. As you adopt this approach, you'll discover that making little, regular progress over time demonstrates that beating procrastination is within your reach - two minutes at a time.

Break
Task
Into
Smaller
Portions
To Conquer
PROCASTINATION

Chapter Two

Tip 2: The Pomodoro Technique.

The struggle to sustain focused productivity in a world full of distractions might feel never-ending. The Pomodoro Technique helps in time management and provides an organized method for completing work while maintaining mental brightness and increasing productivity.

Understanding The Pomodoro Technique

The Pomodoro Technique's core principle is to divide your work into concentrated segments, or "Pomodoros," which are typically 25 minutes long. There is a brief interval of around 5 minutes after each Pomodoro to give your mind a chance to rest. Four sets of Pomodoros are performed before a longer rest of 15 to 30 minutes is taken. This regular cycle aims to minimize the development of mental weariness while maximizing your cognitive powers.

Optimizing Your Method

You might find that the Pomodoro Technique has to be customized as you incorporate it into your daily practice. While certain activities could call for longer periods of concentrated labor, others might call for more regular breaks. One of the advantages of the approach is its adaptability to your working style.

Utilizing Time Management's Power

Timeboxing, or allotting tasks a certain amount of time, is one of the core ideas behind the Pomodoro Technique. You instill a sense of dedication and urgency to the current activity by setting a timer for each Pomodoro. This targeted time management strategy stops procrastination and discourages the propensity to multitask, ensuring that your entire attention is maintained.

When faced with lengthy or difficult activities that could normally feel overwhelming, the Pomodoro Technique is very useful. These activities become more attainable and realizable when they are divided into digestible chunks. You'll feel an increasing feeling of success as you finish each Pomodoro, which will encourage you to keep going.

Focus and Productivity Maintenance

It might be difficult to focus for an extended period in a time of continual connectivity and frequent alerts. The Pomodoro Technique acts as a barrier between you and this diversion. Your only attention is on the work at hand during each Pomodoro. Your cognitive involvement is increased by this immersion, which promotes greater comprehension and more original problem-solving.

Additionally, the frequent, brief intervals provide essential opportunities for mental relaxation. Even a quick break from your work helps you avoid burnout and preserves your mental energy. These breaks also promote a comprehensive perspective on your job, enabling you to assess your progress and change your strategy as necessary.

Defeating Procrastination and Overwhelm

The hazy perception of limitless time is frequently a procrastination booster. The Pomodoro Technique challenges this idea by dividing time into quantifiable components. When given a task, deciding to focus on it for just one Pomodoro sounds less intimidating than committing to it for an extended period. The barrier that causes procrastination may be eliminated with one straightforward mindset change.

The Pomodoro Technique also acts as a safeguard against overwhelm and fatigue. Because of the regular pauses, mental tiredness is prevented from building up. By giving your brain a frequent break, you can keep it functioning at its peak, which will cut down on mistakes and improve the caliber of your work.

Building Self-Control and Mindfulness

In addition to its advantages for time management, the Pomodoro Technique promotes a thoughtful attitude to work. By making a conscious decision to focus on just one job during each Pomodoro, you are prevented from succumbing to the need to divide your attention across several projects. Your work will be more in-depth because of this intense immersion, which also promotes flow.

The Pomodoro Technique also promotes self-control in sticking to your work plan. It allows you to be present in the moment since it serves as a visible reminder that you're allocating set times to work. Your total time management abilities will improve as a result of this discipline, which you acquire through constant practice.

Adapting The Pomodoro Technique

Although a Pomodoro is typically 25 minutes long, it's important to understand that everyone's ideal work period may vary. Try out various time frames to see which one best matches your energy and attention span. Striking a balance between intense labor and restorative breaks is the objective.

The Pomodoro Technique also promotes self-awareness. You may learn more about your peak production times, attention spans, and propensities to get distracted by other things by applying yourself consistently. With this knowledge, you can plan your Pomodoros to coincide with your busiest periods and approach your most difficult chores with foresight.

The Pomodoro Technique involves a change in perspective as well as a plan. It cultivates a focused work ethic while encouraging you to appreciate your time and energy.

The Pomodoro Technique involves taking back control of your time and attention, not merely breaking up the day into manageable chunks. You may achieve more productivity, sharper focus, and a healthier work-life balance by embracing its regulated routine. You'll come to understand that the actual meaning of productivity is found in the quality of your concentrated efforts, rather than the amount of time spent, as you develop your Pomodoro practice and see the transformational benefits of your work.

I can't do this work now maybe Later

Chapter Three

Tip 3: The Procrastination-Action Loop

The act of procrastinating frequently functions like a sneaky cycle that feeds off of our routines and psychological cues. The first step to reclaiming control over your actions and ending the cycle of delay is to recognize and interrupt this loop.

Finding Patterns and Triggers

A collection of triggers that catalyze the process is at the center of the procrastination-action cycle. These triggers may be mental, emotional, or circumstantial Overwhelming emotions, failure, or simply plain boredom are often causes of Procrastination. Understanding your procrastination tendencies begins with recognizing these triggers.

Think about the projects you frequently put off. Is there a pattern to the kinds of jobs you put off? Do specific circumstances or feelings always come before you procrastinate? By seeing these trends, you may gain an understanding of the underlying reasons for your delay and take appropriate action.

Breaking of the Delay Cycle

Disrupting the procrastination loop is the next step after identifying your triggers and habits. This entails deliberate, proactive tactics designed to step in before procrastination gathers steam. "Task chunking" is a useful strategy. Instead of tackling a daunting activity all at once, divide it up into more manageable sections. This stops overwhelm from occurring and makes starting the activity less intimidating.

Another essential component of breaking the circle is mindfulness. Recognize the trigger when you notice yourself on the verge of procrastination. Inhale deeply and decide to focus on the work at hand. This exercise helps you become more self-aware and gives you the ability to shift your attention away from the need to put anything off.

Reframing and Rewarding

Procrastination may be effectively treated by changing the way you see your work. Instead of becoming stuck on the work involved, concentrate on the joy of finishing the task. Imagine the benefits and relief you'll have after finishing the assignment. Your brain is rewired by this mentality change to correlate the job with a successful conclusion, which lowers the start-up resistance.

Implementing a system of rewards can also give people the drive to start acting. Establish a little incentive for yourself when you finish a chore you've been putting off. Procrastination's grip is loosened as a result of this encouraging reinforcement, which strengthens the link between action and satisfaction.

The regularity and contentment that the procrastination-action loop relies on predictability

You can destroy the foundation that procrastination is built on by recognizing triggers, and patterns, and intentionally breaking the loop. You are actively regaining your agency over your duties through intentional interventions, rephrasing, and conscious redirection.

Keep in mind that perseverance and practice are necessary to break the procrastination cycle. You'll find yourself better able to go from delay to action as you develop your ability to identify your triggers and use efficient techniques. You are developing a mindset that is ready for productivity and equipped to take on even the most difficult tasks with each successful disruption of the loop.

When?

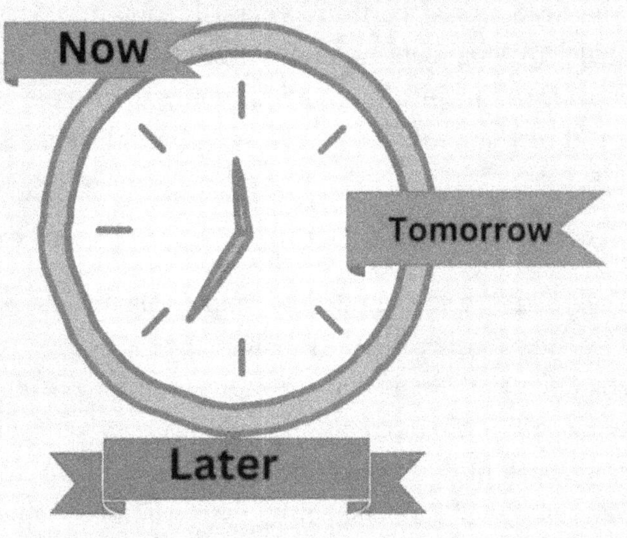

Chapter Four

Tip 4: Visualization and Goal Setting

A distinct feeling of purpose and direction is frequently what leads someone from procrastination to success. The value of goal-setting and visualization rests in their capacity to inspire motivation, concentrate your efforts, and direct you toward significant accomplishments.

Setting up definite, compelling goals

Your activities are guided by your goals, which give you a feeling of direction. However, not all objectives are created equal. Goals that are vague or uninteresting might encourage procrastination because they lack the emotional pull that will motivate you to go forward. Setting SMART (specific, measurable, attainable, relevant, and time-bound) objectives is crucial.

When creating your objectives, create a clear picture of the result you want. Instead of stating a goal like "Exercise more," for example, make it more interesting by saying "Complete 5,000 runs in three months." This precision helps you visualize achievement and increases your will to act.

How to Increase Motivation through Visualization

Visualization is a potent tool that makes use of the mind's capacity to conjure up scenarios. You may train your brain to see something as possible and desirable by vividly seeing yourself completing a task or reaching a goal. This in turn increases your drive to take action.

Close your eyes for a few minutes each day and see yourself accomplishing the activities you've been putting off. Imagine the sense of pride, the joy, and the material benefits that come from doing these duties. Your brain is set up for action when you visualize, which significantly lowers your resistance to beginning.

- Putting together a vision board; By making a vision board, you may improve visualization with a practical approach. Gather pictures, words, and other symbols that speak to your desires. Put them on a board that you can easily see every day, whether it be real or digital. Your goals are reinforced by this visible reminder, which also acts as a continual source of inspiration
- Engage with your vision board frequently, especially when you are tempted to put off anything. Your brain is stimulated by the visual clues to link your actions with the results you want, which makes it harder to rationalize waiting.

Setting goals and using visualization are powerful strategies for overcoming procrastination. They give your work a meaning and give your actions a purpose. The once-daunting duties will transform into stepping stones toward realizing your objectives as you hone your goal-setting techniques and include visualization in your daily routine.

Keep in mind that in the fight against procrastination, your mind is a strong friend. You may rewire your brain to see activities as chances for development, achievement, and personal fulfillment by developing a clear picture of your goals and regularly picturing your success.

Do the things you dread and dread will go away

Chapter Five

Tip 5: The Power of Accountability

An organized approach and outside assistance are frequently helpful while navigating the world of productivity. The strength of accountability rests in its capacity to keep you on course, uphold your dedication, and translate your goals into actionable steps.

Getting Other People's Help

Accountability's social component gives it power. When you tell someone else about your objectives and commitments, you add an outside influence that motivates you to take action. Select a dependable accountability partner, committed to your progress, and helpful. The person in question may be a friend, coworker, mentor, or even a coach.

Check-ins with your accountability partner regularly instill a feeling of accountability. Your dedication to your goals increases when you are aware that you will be reporting your progress. This civic responsibility can act as a potent inhibitor of procrastination, encouraging you to move consistently in the direction of your goals.

Monitoring Results and Remaining Committed

Tracking systems work best when they are linked with accountability. Implement a system for tracking your progress, whether it's a paper planner, an online program, or a straightforward to-do list. Inform your accountability partner regularly of your successes, failures, and difficulties. The process of tracking helps you stay focused on your objectives and strengthens your will to achieve them.

Think about establishing checkpoints along the way as well. These are more manageable goals that show your development. Celebrating these achievements not only increases your drive but also gives you a chance to evaluate the success of your plan. To make sure you continue on the path of constant activity, adjust your strategy as necessary.

Developing Accountability System

Consider joining a club or community that has similar objectives if you're seeking a more structured approach to responsibility. These communities, whether they are mastermind groups, workshops, or online forums, offer a built-in support system. Surrounding yourself with others who share your desire for success and productivity may greatly strengthen your will to act.

Keep in mind that accountability is about encouraging progress, not passing judgment. It's a recognition that improvement requires regular work and that encouragement from others may give you the little push you need to beat procrastination.

The ability to take responsibility is inextricably linked to the reality that people thrive in collaborative environments that promote success. You actively support your dedication to your goals by soliciting the help of others and incorporating tracking methods. You are gradually turning your ambitions into reality via accountability.

Accept external cues, acknowledge your successes, and see setbacks as chances to improve. Accountability is a mentality shift that strengthens your commitment to take action, not merely a tool. You'll discover as you progress down this path that responsibility increases output, promotes a feeling of community, and energizes your pursuit of achievement.

Time waits for Nobody so start now! and don't push it to Later.

Chapter Six

Tip 6. Embracing Imperfection

The fear of falling short of expectations or striving for perfection are common causes of procrastination. To overcome procrastination, you must learn to embrace imperfection. This will release you from the grip of fear and allow you to continue growing.

Getting Past fear of Failure

Perfection may be a crippling quest. When you hold yourself to unattainable standards, the worry of failing might keep you from beginning a work altogether. One of the most deadly foes of procrastination is the dread of failure.

Reframing failure as a stepping stone to achievement is a necessary component of accepting imperfection. Recognize that errors and failures are chances for growth rather than indicators of weakness. By changing your viewpoint, you eliminate procrastination's main motivator—the worry that you won't be perfect.

Allowing yourself the space to develop

Putting off taking action while you wait for the "perfect" opportunity or the "perfect" strategy is a common cause of procrastination. You may escape this trap by accepting imperfection. Recognize that perfection is an illusion and that waiting for the perfect situation might result in missed chances and unreached objectives.

Instead, give priority to action above accuracy. Recognize that while your earliest attempts may not have been perfect, they are nevertheless crucial first steps. Regardless of the outcome, every attempt teaches you something useful that advances your development. You're moving forward and strengthening your resistance to procrastination by acting and enabling yourself to learn from your mistakes.

Having reasonable goals

Although pursuing greatness is admirable, perfectionism is its destructive relative. Realistic expectations need a grasp of your limitations and the nonlinear nature of advancement. Set reasonable goals along the road and divide activities into digestible pieces. Even if your development isn't perfect, acknowledge it.

Keep in mind that progress occurs when you push yourself past your comfort zone and overcome obstacles. You're giving yourself permission to take chances and venture into uncharted territory by accepting imperfection. Even imperfect steps forward help you grow as a person and gradually loosen procrastination's hold on you.

Accepting imperfection does not call for carelessness or indifference. It's a challenge to have bravery and recognize that making errors and learning from them are both necessary for advancement. You may neutralize procrastination's main tool, fear, by letting go of the demand for perfection and establishing a growth-oriented mentality.

As you internalize this viewpoint and take action without the crippling burden of perfectionism, you'll discover that you're more motivated to start projects, try new things, and rise to obstacles. The transition from procrastination to productivity shifts the focus from avoiding errors to seizing possibilities for growth, evolution, and eventually meaningful success.

**You
Miss
100%
Of
The
Shots
You
Don't
Take**

Chapter Seven

Tip 7: Mindfulness and proactive action

Being aware stands out as a powerful cure for procrastination in a world of continual distractions and information overload. The attraction of delay may be successfully resisted by practicing present-moment awareness and carefully selecting your activities, which will also increase your total productivity.

Increasing Present-Moment Awareness

Being present and involved in the here and now is the practice of mindfulness. It entails objectively evaluating your thoughts, feelings, and environment. When it comes to procrastination, mindfulness may assist you in identifying the small indicators that cause delay, such as a transient want to check social media or a brief feeling of insecurity.

Start by including mindfulness in your regular activities. Spend a few minutes each day concentrating only on your breath, feelings, or thoughts. As you get better at doing this, you'll become more aware of the thoughts and behaviors that lead to procrastination, which will help you stop it before it gets out of control.

Making Conscious Decisions to Act

Procrastination frequently entails unthinking, automatic reactions to cues. You get the ability to break this habitual pattern and make informed decisions through mindfulness. If you find yourself inclined to put off a chore, take a moment to consider your options. Is it really necessary to take a break, or is it just an avoidance strategy brought on by procrastination?

You regain control over your behavior by making deliberate decisions. You're deliberately choosing to engage with the work at hand rather than giving in to the impulse to put it off. Procrastination's hold eventually erodes as a result of this transition from reactive behavior to deliberate action.

How to Use Mindfulness in Tasks

The actual performance of activities might incorporate mindfulness as well. Be more conscious of your actions and the process as you work. Avoid multitasking and give each activity your entire attention. This not only increases productivity but also gives you a sense of pleasure and success, which fights the temptation of procrastination.

Additionally, mindfulness stops rumination, which is the propensity to brood over the past or worry about the future. You may take action more easily by reducing stress and overload by keeping your attention on the current moment.

Clarity, attention, and intentionality are all qualities that may be developed via mindfulness, which is more than just a technique. Adopting mindfulness in your productivity strategy removes the procrastinating automatic response and enables you to make informed decisions.

You'll notice that the distance between intention and action gets less as you continue to practice mindfulness. You'll learn more about yourself and improve your ability to spot the instances when procrastination tries to take over. By incorporating mindfulness into your behaviors, you're cultivating a greater feeling of presence, purpose, and efficacy in many areas of your life in addition to overcoming procrastination.

today is the day
to
Slay Procrastination

Chapter Eight

Tip 8: Productivity and the Environment

Your capacity to fend against procrastination and boost productivity can be strongly impacted by the workplace environment. You may create an environment in your office that encourages concentration, reduces interruptions, and increases productivity.

Your capacity to focus and participate in work is significantly influenced by your environment. Start by cleaning your physical workspace. Clear out your desk, organize your resources in an orderly manner, and check the lighting. Clear thinking is encouraged and visual distractions are lessened in a clutter-free setting.

Beyond physical organization, think about how your workstation is set up. Place your computer, monitor, and other necessary equipment to reduce strain and promote a smooth workflow. Decorate your environment with things that uplift you, whether they be artwork, plants, or inspirational phrases.

Reducing interruptions and increasing productivity

Productivity is ruined by distractions. Make a conscious effort to reduce any distractions you know will slow you down, whether they be alerts, social media, or outside noise. Use website blockers, disable unused notifications, or set up a targeted work schedule.

Utilize technology to your advantage by blocking distracting websites with Apps when you need to concentrate. Put your phone in "do not disturb" mode or set aside certain hours to check social media and communications. You may create a road to undistracted work by taking proactive measures to manage your digital surroundings.

Making a dedicated workspace helps to further block out distractions. Inform individuals around you about your devoted work hours to demonstrate your dedication to targeted action. If your surroundings are noisy, think about investing in noise-canceling headphones, and set up clear limits to ward against disruptions.

Additionally, ergonomics are very important for productivity. Your physical well-being and ability to concentrate on work are improved by using a comfortable chair, an adjustable desk, and the right arrangement of your keyboard and monitor.

Try out several features in your workstation to determine which ones increase productivity. Color schemes, climate control, and even background music may be examples of this. The goal is to foster an atmosphere that fosters focus and promotes initiative.

Establish a Digital Environment Free of Distractions

The virtual world is equally as significant in the digital era as the real one. Organize your files, folders, and desktops to make your digital workspace more efficient. Remove yourself from unnecessary email lists, then empty your inbox. Organize projects and due dates using tools to make sure nothing gets missed.

Your office serves as a blank canvas for productivity rather than just a physical location. You are actively reducing the procrastination triggers by purposefully designing your surroundings to promote attention and productivity. Your workstation turns into a haven of productivity, where interruptions are kept to a minimum and your dedication to output is sustained.

Keep in mind that designing the perfect workstation is a continuous process. Keep an eye on your surroundings and adapt as necessary to meet your changing demands. Your capacity to commence projects and keep prolonged attention will become second nature as you fine-tune your workstation, giving you the ability to beat procrastination and easily achieve your goals.

A joyful and enthusiastic environment promotes a positive outlook and lessens the probability of procrastination.

PROCRASTINATION IS A HABIT NOT A PERSONALITY TRAIT

Chapter Nine

Tip 9: Finding intrinsic Motivation

The strength of intrinsic motivation, the drive that pushes you to take action because of personal satisfaction and fulfillment, is at the core of beating procrastination. You may light a fire within yourself that motivates you to overcome procrastination and persistently pursue your objectives by discovering your intrinsic sources of passion and purpose.

Recognizing intrinsic Motivation

Intrinsic motivation is a form of drive that originates inside. Instead of being motivated by incentives or pressure from others, it is driven by your personal interests, values, and passions. When you are intrinsically driven, it is simpler to get started and keep going since the act of doing the activity is enjoyable in and of itself.

Finding your intrinsic drive entails identifying what you truly love, what is consistent with your beliefs, and what gives your life meaning. This emotional connection to your work acts as a natural inhibitor of procrastination since the pleasure and satisfaction it brings transcend any reluctance to begin.

Think about the things you've been putting off. Consider why these responsibilities are important to you personally. How do they advance your objectives, principles, or development? Your chores become meaningful activities by taking on a deeper significance, converting them from routine obligations.

Instead of seeing exercise as a duty, consider it a chance to prioritize your health and well-being. Similarly, when working on a project at work, consider how completion may affect your career path or improve your professional abilities.

You may encourage intrinsic motivation to grow if you understand the importance of each work in the overall scheme of your life. You may provide a task intrinsic motivation by linking it to a worthwhile result. Your readiness to act differently as a result of this perspective shift.

Using enthusiasm and purpose

Passion and purpose are significant intrinsic motivational factors. Find the things in your life that make you passionate; those things, people, or causes that make you feel alive and inspired. When you match your responsibilities with your interests, they stop being burdens and turn into occasions to indulge in what makes you happy.

Additionally, it gives jobs a deeper sense of significance by tying them to your main life mission. You're more likely to see them as crucial stages in your path when you understand how each activity adds to your long-term goals. The attraction of procrastination is defeated by this more comprehensive viewpoint.

Including Internal Motivation

Choosing chores that align with your beliefs, interests, and passions is a deliberate step in incorporating intrinsic motivation into your daily routine. Look for assignments that will let you utilize your talents. To make jobs more attainable and realizable, divide larger activities into smaller, more manageable segments.

Honor the work you're doing on activities that are important to you by celebrating your progress along the way. Your link to intrinsic motivation is strengthened with each step you take, becoming a driving force in your quest for productivity.

A strong ally in the fight against procrastination, intrinsic motivation transfers your attention from outside demands to internal sources of satisfaction. You may cultivate a mentality that values proactive action by identifying personal motivations for taking action, engaging your interests, and connecting activities to your purpose.

Promoting Growth Mindset

As mentioned in earlier suggestions, intrinsic motivation is intimately related to having a development mentality. Accept the idea that work and learning may help you improve your skills and intellect over time. This way of thinking enables you to see difficulties not as obstacles but as chances to develop and learn.

Remind yourself that challenges and setbacks are a necessary part of the trip whenever you encounter them. Approach them with an open mind and a desire to learn. You may foster intrinsic drive and increase resilience in the face of procrastination and hardship by adopting a growth mindset.

Mindful Participation

The cultivation of intrinsic motivation is significantly aided by mindfulness, as was discussed in Tip 7. When you perform work consciously, you are focused on the task at hand. You may appreciate the subtleties of each work and uncover secret layers of happiness and fulfillment thanks to your increased awareness.

As you complete your duties practice mindfulness by monitoring your thoughts and emotions without passing judgment. Immerse yourself in the activity by using all of your senses. You may cultivate intrinsic motivation by encouraging this attentive engagement, which is the pure delight of being fully engaged in what you're doing.

The barrier to starting chores will decrease as you infuse them with intrinsic drive. The pleasure, satisfaction, and sense of achievement you get from completing the activities themselves becomes your motivation to move on. Keep in mind that your internal motivation is a source of power that may keep you moving forward even when other elements are uncertain. You are giving your trip purpose and vigor as you continuously match your responsibilities with your values and passions. When you use intrinsic motivation as your driving force, you don't merely beat procrastination—instead, you embrace a life of fulfillment, advancement, and significant achievement.

Procrastination
Steals
Time

Summary

Procrastination, though a persistent adversary, is not an insurmountable one. Armed with the insights and strategies from the nine tips discussed in this guide, you're well-equipped to break free from its grip and embark on a journey of increased productivity, achievement, and personal growth.

From understanding the power of the Two-Minute Rule to harnessing the Pomodoro Technique, identifying triggers and patterns of the Procrastination-Action Loop, and embracing imperfection, you've explored a diverse toolkit for combating procrastination. You've also delved into the realms of mindfulness, accountability, intrinsic motivation, and the importance of an optimized environment.

Remember that progress is a gradual process, and setbacks are part of the journey. Approach your quest to overcome procrastination with patience, self-compassion, and a growth mindset. As you implement these strategies, you're not just transforming your approach to tasks; you're cultivating a mindset that thrives on action, resilience, and achievement.

Therefore you must commit to lasting change.

Each tip is like a puzzle piece that contributes to the larger picture of your productivity journey. The interplay of these strategies strengthens your resolve, refines your focus, and empowers you to rise above the allure of delay.

As you navigate the challenges, embrace setbacks, and celebrate victories, you're forging a path toward personal excellence.

Ultimately, conquering procrastination is not just about getting things done – it's about reclaiming your time, your potential, and your sense of agency. Armed with the tools from this guide, you're taking control of your actions, cultivating a mindset of purpose and determination, and embracing a life characterized by accomplishment and fulfillment.

So, as you embark on this transformative journey, may these nine surprising tips serve as beacons of guidance, inspiration, and motivation. Here's to a future where action takes precedence, where goals are realized, and where the cycle of procrastination is replaced with a cycle of productivity, growth, and success.

Apps and Productivity Tools

- **Todoist** is a task management app that uses tools like due dates, reminders, and project labels to help you organize your chores and projects.

- **Forest** is an app that promotes concentration by allowing you to plant virtual trees that grow when you avoid using your phone and other sources of distraction.
- **Trello** is a visual collaboration tool that lets you set up boards, lists, and cards to organize tasks, projects, and objectives.

- **Focus@Will** is a music software that plays background music that has been scientifically shown to improve attention in order to increase focus and productivity.

- **RescueTime** A time-tracking tool that tracks your digital activity and gives you insights into how you spend your time.

- **Freedom** is a website and app blocker that keeps you concentrated at work by preventing access to distracting websites and applications.

Keep in mind that these tools are there to support you on your path, and you may personalize your strategy by looking into the ones that speak to you the most. In order to better comprehend procrastination and further your search for greater levels of productivity and personal fulfillment, each resource offers particular insights and methods.

www.ingramcontent.com/pod-product-compliance
Lightning Source LLC
Chambersburg PA
CBHW071112260726
48661CB00006B/2588

* 9 7 9 8 8 6 0 4 6 1 0 6 2 *